YOUR KNOWLEDGE HAS VALUE

- We will publish your bachelor's and master's thesis, essays and papers

- Your own eBook and book - sold worldwide in all relevant shops

- Earn money with each sale

Upload your text at www.GRIN.com and publish for free

Bibliographic information published by the German National Library:

The German National Library lists this publication in the National Bibliography; detailed bibliographic data are available on the Internet at http://dnb.dnb.de .

Imprint:

Copyright © 2016 GRIN Verlag, Open Publishing GmbH
Print and binding: Books on Demand GmbH, Norderstedt Germany
ISBN: 9783668450158

This book at GRIN:

http://www.grin.com/en/e-book/365529/what-is-the-effect-of-the-brexit-on-the-economy-of-the-united-kingdom-and

Thomas Schaaf

What is the effect of the Brexit on the economy of the United Kingdom and the European Union?

GRIN Publishing

GRIN - Your knowledge has value

Since its foundation in 1998, GRIN has specialized in publishing academic texts by students, college teachers and other academics as e-book and printed book. The website www.grin.com is an ideal platform for presenting term papers, final papers, scientific essays, dissertations and specialist books.

Visit us on the internet:

http://www.grin.com/

http://www.facebook.com/grincom

http://www.twitter.com/grin_com

What is the effect of the Brexit on the economy of the United Kingdom and the European Union?

Gesamtschule Niederzier/Merzenich

Thomas Schaaf

Table of Content

1. Introduction

On June 23rd 2016 the whole world had its eyes on the Great Britain, anxious to know whether or not the Britons would vote for the "Brexit", which stands for the end of the British membership in the European Union. After weeks of "YES" and "NO" campaigns, the vote decided that 51,9 % of the British people wanted their country to leave the European Union.

In the following I will explain what the word Brexit means and shortly outline the course of events from the passage of the law for the referendum until the actual leave. Then I will take a closer look at the effects on the economy of Great Britain and the EU. I will structure this part into three fractions of time, describing the period before the referendum, the period between the referendum and the point of the exit and the time after the exit.[1]

2. General Information

2.1 Definition of "Brexit"

The word "Brexit" is a combination of the words "Britain" and "exit". A similar word creation,"Grexit", was first introduced by the press for the possible exit of Greece out of the European Union during their financial crisis. This was now changed into "Brexit" as a short form for the United Kingdom leaving the European Union. [2]

2.2 Timeline of the Brexit

In January 2013 the British Prime Minister David Cameron announced that in case of his re-election in May 2015 he would hold a Referendum about the topic if the United Kingdom should stay in the European Union. The deadline for this Referendum was set for the year 2017. The main reason for this step was that the British UKIP, an EU-critical party, had rising survey results.

---

[1] Cf. Source 1
[2] Cf. Source 1

David Cameron finally introduced a law concerning the EU-referendum into Parliament which was passed in December 2015.

End of February 2016 David Cameron announced the referendum to take place on June 23rd 2016. On this day 33 million Britons went to the ballot boxes. 51,9 % of them voted for the exit.

The next day Cameron declared his resign as Prime Minister, on July 23rd former Home Secretary Theresa May became his successor.

It is on her and her party now to plan and present the steps towards the British leave. It is expected that the negotiations for the exit will start in spring 2017. Once started Article 50 of the Treaty on European Union rules that the process of leaving has to be concluded within two years. So the point of leave will most likely be in the year 2019.[3]

3. Development of the United Kingdom's and European Union's economy until the referendum

3.1 Impacts on the United Kingdom

During the last twelve months before the vote took place, economic growth slowed down from 0,6 % to 0,4 %.[4] The growing uncertainty concerning the outcome and the possible consequences lead to postponing of investments and shifting money from the riskier stock markets to saver forms of investments like gold or annuity certificates. The Financial Times Stock Exchange 100 index (FTSE) which includes the one hundred strongest papers traded at the London Stock Exchange also shows that the British economy got weaker as the date for the exit vote came closer. Within the last twelve months before the vote the FTSE dropped from more than seven thousand points to close to six thousand. [5]

---

[3] Cf. Source 1
[4] Cf. Source 9
[5] Cf. Source 2

Chart: Development of the FTSE during the last 3 years[6]

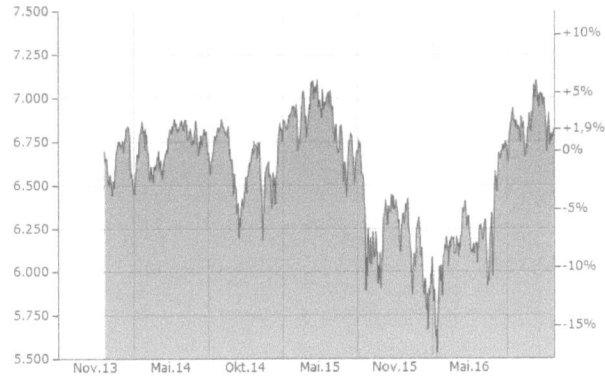

Chart: Currency Exchange Rate British Pound – USD (1 year)[7]

3.2 Effects on the economy of the European Union

Like the FTSE the European counterpart, the EURO STOXX 50 index has gone down significantly before the Brexit vote was made.

The EURO STOXX 50 is a stock index which includes fifty leading stocks of the Euro-zone. As can be seen in the EURO STOXX 50 chart, the stock exchange fell ever since the referendum has been announced. On the one hand this decrease is based on uncertainty and fears of European investors and brokers. On the other it was likely be caused by brokers and

---

[6] Cf. Source 3
[7] Cf. Source 4

investors who built risk into a stock to prevent a dramatic crash of the market. Notwithstanding the tension between the EU and the UK, the Euro has been a stable currency on the market compared to the Pound and has also been on an increase in the past couple of years. The fact that Europeans didn't believe in the Euro being a stable stock can be seen as a reason for it being as stable as it used to be.[8]

Chart: EURO STOXX 50 (1 year period)[9]

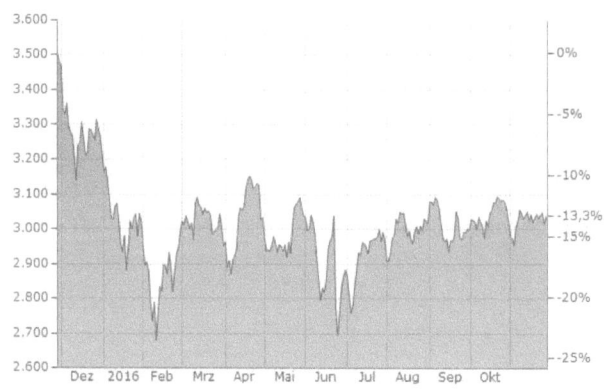

Chart: Currency Exchange Rate Euro-Dollar (1 year period)[10]

---

[8] Cf. Source 5
[9] Cf. Source 6
[10] Cf. Source 7

6

4. Development of the United Kingdom´s and European Union´s economy from the referendum to the exit

4.1. Implication on the United Kingdom

4.1.1. General economical situation

The time after the referendum was marked by uncertainty. The overall economic atmosphere was pessimistic with declining business activities. Companies and investors who were thinking on investing in the United Kingdom stopped their plans to wait until it would become clear what the relationship between the United Kingdom and the EU will look like. To encourage new investments and strengthen the economy the Bank of England reduced its key interest rates in August.[11] The British government announced to lower corporate taxes to attract foreign companies.[12] So at the end of the year 2016 the economic growth and business activities are at a lower level as at the beginning of the year but the effects of the referendum are not at all as significant as analysts had predicted.

For the remaining time until the final leave much depends on the structure the relationship between the UK and the EU finally will have.

4.1.2. Financial markets

On the day after the referendum the British Pound dropped dramatically and lost almost 11 percent of its value compared to the US Dollar and the Euro. Until today its value sank continuously and no imminent raise is expected.

The FTSE in contrary only suffered a loss of about 3 % on that day. Until now the index could gain back its former losses, staying now at around 7000 points again.[13]

Many worldwide operating British enterprises profit from the weak Pound. Shell, for example, sells the oil that is produced in dollar and exchanges its income into Pounds. So a barrel of oil that is sold for thirty US Dollars was worth about fifteen Pounds before the Brexit. Now they receive about 20 Pounds for the same amount of oil.

---

[11] Cf. Source 8
[12] Cf. Source 10
[13] Cf. Source 2

This effect is only based on currency exchange gains but it leads to significant profits for some mayor British companies. Especially companies producing export goods or services are prospering.

On the other side, companies that rely on imports or supplies from outside of the United Kingdom suffer. The British airline Easy Jet for example loses profit because they sell many of their flight tickets on the British markets in British Pounds but most of their costs have to be paid in US Dollars like fuel or fees.[14]

4.2. Impacts on the European Union

4.2.1. General economical situation

After the first disquiet weeks the situation calmed down. Already existing businesses continued as for the referendum. But new investments into the British market were and still are stopped or postponed as it is unclear how the economic relationship between the UK and the EU will look like. Companies that already have strong business links to the United Kingdom are busy working on plans on how to continue their businesses under the different exit scenarios. This applies for example to the German automobile producer BMW, whose brand "Mini" is produced in Great Britain.[15]

Although no hard impact on the European economy can be seen today and the situation within the companies seems to be calm, underneath the surface a lot is going on as the enterprises try to prepare for the new economic situation.

4.2.2. Financial Markets

The day after the referendum was announced the European stock market crashed dramatically. Alongside the EURO STOXX 50 many other stocks, especially at the German, Spanish and Italian markets dropped about 10%. After the first agitated weeks after the decision, the stock market stabilized itself and the currency exchange rate of the Euro to Dollar has settled down to a more even state.[16]

---

[14] Cf. Source 11
[15] Cf. Source 12
[16] Cf. Source 2

5. Development of the United Kingdom´s and European Union´s economy after the exit

5.1. The United Kingdom as an "EEC State"
5.1.1. Main aspects of the EEA Agreement

As of today Norway, Switzerland, Iceland and Liechtenstein are member states of the European Free Trade Association, EFTA. Norway, Iceland and Liechtenstein build the European Economic Community, EEC, together with the European Union. The rules and conditions of this association were fixed in the EEA Agreement. Therefore these three countries are also called the EFTA EEA States.

The EEA Agreement basically extends the Single Market of the European Union to these countries. It allows free movement of goods, services, capital and persons. Trade barriers such as customs, taxes, and regulations are disposed or at least limited.[17]

However, the EFTA EEA States have no right to decide on new laws within the EU, but they are obliged to give financial aid to the new EU member states to "reduce economic and social disparities".[18] The amount Norway contributes in the years 2014 to 2021 adds up to 1.250 million Euro.[19]

5.1.2. Consequences for the British economy under the EEA Agreement

As the conditions for the trade of goods and services are more or less the same for EFTA EEA States and EU member states, the impacts on the economy of the United Kingdom would be light. Only minor adjustments would be necessary, for example because of different rules for value added taxes (VAT). Because of that the economy of the United Kingdom would most likely stay stable, economic growth would increase continuously.

On the other hand most of the mayor concerns of the UK regarding the EU membership would not be solved either. The EEA Agreement allows the free movement of citizens in order to find work and live wherever they want. So under the EEA Agreement the British government could not follow their plans to reduce and control immigration. In addition to that the United Kingdom would be obliged to give financial support to the European Union. On

---

[17] Cf. Source 14
[18] Cf. Source 13
[19] Cf. Source 13

top of that the UK would not take part in the decision on new rules within the single market any longer.

Co-signing an already existing and introduced contract like the EEA Agreement gives security to both sides. Everybody knows what to expect. So at the moment the United Kingdom decides to sign the Agreement the time of uncertainty for the British economy ends and the companies can start to adjust their businesses to the new rules.

Summed up, signing the EEA Agreement would not bring significant new developments in the economic surrounding and no solution to pressing matters of the British economy but would be the easiest to implement.

5.1.3. Impacts on the economy of the European Union

For the economy of the European Union the changes would almost be non-significant if the United Kingdom should sign the EEA Agreement. The rules and regulations are already known and are more or less the same as for EU member states. It might even make decisions easier as the United Kingdom often was a partner who slowed down or even stopped developments with its concerns.

So, on the European side, too, no mayor impacts are to be expected.

5.2. The United Kingdom as an EFTA State with bilateral Agreements
5.2.1. The Swiss Model

Switzerland is the one EFTA State that has not signed the EEA Agreement. Therefore the relationship between Switzerland and the European Union and the principles for trade are defined through different agreements. The Free Trade Agreement allows customs free trade of industrial products, the Agreement on movement of goods simplifies border control and formalities. The Bilaterale I and II Agreements further opened the markets, eased trading conditions and allowed the free movement of persons between the EU and Switzerland. Several other contracts were signed to ease the market access for separate branches, like aviation or transportation.

Switzerland, too, contributes money to support the new EU member states. The financial aid amounts to 130 million Francs a year.[20]

---

[20] Cf. Source 15

5.2.2. The possible consequences for the UK

The EFTA outlines certain standards for the trade of services and goods, but beside this, agreements need to be negotiated for every area of the economy where cross-border businesses are involved. Otherwise trade between the EU and the UK would be more difficult. For example when there are no agreements on customs procedures, taxation rules, or safety standards.

It becomes even more difficult in areas where the EU and the UK have different interests, like in the financial sector. Until now, London is the most important financial market in Europe, followed by Frankfurt, Madrid and Milan. The British government will fight for the position of their capital London whereas the EU might be much more interested in strengthening their own financial centers.[21]

So in many areas the outcome of the negotiations is totally open. This will keep the British economy in a state of uncertainty and standstill. The companies will wait until after the agreements have been signed before further investing in business activities.

Even after that the economy of the United Kingdom will still be unsettled as the companies need time to adjust to the new conditions and possibly rearrange their business activities.

5.2.3. Impacts on the European Economy

On the EU side, too, businesses with and investments in the United Kingdom will be cancelled or at least postponed until it becomes clear what the rules and regulations for cross-border activities will look like. EU companies might shift planned investments to other EU countries where the conditions are clear. And they will look for new markets within the European Union too.

Overall it is easier for EU-companies to find new business partners and markets for their products as it is for British companies as they act under a solid legal system. Because of this, foreign companies will also be more interested in starting businesses in the EU than in the UK.

All this would most likely lead to an increase of the economic growth in the EU.

---

[21] Cf. Source 16

5.3. The United Kingdom as an independent European state

5.3.1. Basic outlines of the economic relationships

For an independent European state like for example Russia, none of
the agreements that exist within the EU, the EFTA or the EEC will
apply. In order to generate good conditions for the trade of goods and
services several bilateral agreements are in force between different countries respectively the
EU and different countries; for example contracts on customs unions, free trade agreements or
treaties concerning import and export, economical corporation or access-rights to ports and
airports.

The World Trade Organization WTO defines standards to reduce trade barriers and customs
regulations, to prevent discriminatory treatment of foreign products and to harmonize trade
regulations between the member states. [22]

5.3.2. Consequences for the United Kingdom

It is not even clear if the UK would still be a member of the WTO because they signed the
contract as a member of the EU which they no longer would be. As these rules are on a very
general level, the UK would be forced to sign single agreements with every country or the EU
separately if they want to improve and ease their economic relationships.[23]

If the United Kingdom would not stay a member of the WTO automatically, this would
increase the number of contracts needed. All this would need a lot of time which would leave
the British economy in a situation without reliable rules for a long time. Negotiations between
business partners or investigations to enter the markets will become more difficult. Most
likely, the growth rate in the UK would decline until a new system of trade agreements would
be introduced.

5.3.3. The position of the European Union

For the European Union the United Kingdom would become a trade partner like any other
country outside the European Economic Community. As the UK would no longer be a
privileged partner, there would be no reason for the EU to priorities negotiations with the UK

---

[22] Cf. Source 17-19
[23] Cf. Source 20

or to allow special conditions for the UK. Most likely the European enterprises would already have looked for other opportunities for their commercial operations and have sought new markets for their products and services.

So even if the economy of the EU might suffer for a while and economic growth could decline, in the long term the effect of the British exit would not be permanent and the European economy would recover.

6. Outlook for the Future

Considering all aspects, the most likely scenario is that the United Kingdom would become an independent state. EFTA and EEA are no suitable options for the United Kingdom. Looking at Norway and Switzerland, both countries allow the free movement of persons and contribute considerable amounts of money to the EU as a price to have access to the European single market. So many things just stay the same for the UK. The British population and the British government would not accept such conditions because their mayor issues like uncontrolled immigration and high payments to the EU would not be solved.

Staying in the European single market but not accepting the other conditions would most likely not be possible either. German Chancellor Angela Merkel already pointed out that the EU would not allow "cherry picking"[24] which means that the UK could either accept contracts like Norway or Switzerland or would have to leave the single market. The EU is afraid that if they would allow the UK these alleviations, other EU members would start thinking of leaving the EU too.

Summing up all this, the only possible way out for the United Kingdom would be a hard Brexit. This means that new contracts with many countries and the EU need to be negotiated and signed. This would take time, especially as the UK for many possible contract partners would be just one of many and not the first in line, as President Barack Obama stated.[25]

The businesses of the United Kingdom and of the European Union will suffer because of the Brexit and lose some of their power. But both, the UK and the EU have a strong economy with well trained work-force, stable political systems and innovative enterprises. So in the long run they will recover and gain their strength again.

---

[24] Cf. Source 21
[25] Cf. Source 22

In the meantime it would be wise to act by the motto of the famous World War II poster from the British Government:[26]

[26] Cf. Source 23

List of References

1. https://de.wikipedia.org/wiki/EU-Austritt_des_Vereinigten_K%C3%B6nigreichs 19:15 6.11.2016

2. http://boerse.ard.de/marktberichte/anleger-unter-brexit-schock100.html 19:45 06.12.2016

3. http://www.finanzen.net/index/FTSE_100 19:59 06.12.2016

4. http://www.finanzen.net/devisen/britische_pfund-us_dollar-kurs 20:01 06.12.2016

5. https://de.wikipedia.org/wiki/EURO_STOXX_50 20:05 06.12.2016

6. http://www.finanzen.net/index/Euro_Stoxx_50 20:07 06.12.2016

7. http://www.finanzen.net/devisen/dollarkurs 20:10 06.12.2016

8. http://www.heute.de/nach-brexit-in-grossbritannien-sorgen-um-platzen-der-immobilienblase-am-finanzplatz-london-44280006.html 20:12 06.12.2016

9. http://www.dw.com/de/gro%C3%9Fbritannien-das-wachstum-wird-schw%C3%A4cher/a-19217783 20:20 06.12.2016

10. http://www.spiegel.de/wirtschaft/soziales/brexit-theresa-may-will-konzerne-radikal-entlasten-a-1122287.html 21:05 15.11.2016

11. https://deutsche-wirtschafts-nachrichten.de/2016/11/15/easyjet-erzielt-weniger-gewinn/ 18:09 27.11.2016

12. http://www.fr-online.de/brexit/automobilbranche-nach-brexit-brexit-bringt-bmw-in-verzwickte-lage,34340058,34419786.html 20:28 06.12.2016

13. http://eeagrants.org/ 19:55 01.12.2016

14. http://www.efta.int/print/1314 15:37 30.11.2016

15. https://www.eda.admin.ch/content/dam/eda/de/documents/publications/EuropaeischeAngelegenheiten/FS-Bilaterale_de.pdf 19:11 30.11.2016

16. http://www.bpb.de/internationales/europa/brexit/229499/folgen-fuer-den-finanzsektor 19:20 30.11.2016

17. https://de.wikipedia.org/wiki/Zollunion 17:17 30.11:2016

18. https://de.wikipedia.org/wiki/Freihandelsabkommen 17:18 30.11.2016

19. https://de.wikipedia.org/wiki/Welthandelsorganisation 17:19 30.11.2016

20. http://uk.reuters.com/article/uk-britain-eu-trade-idUKKBN13U1GT 19:49 01.12.2016

21. https://www.welt.de/politik/deutschland/article156631505/Mit-Merkel-wird-es-kein-Rosinenpicken-fuer-die-Briten-geben.html 20:56 06.12.2016

22. https://www.tagesschau.de/ausland/obama-617.html 20:58 06.12.2016

23. http://www.winstonchurchill.org/resources/in-the-media/churchill-in-the-news/1405-keep-calm-and-carry-on-the-real-story 21:00 06.12.2016

24. https://www.heartbeatinternational.org/keep-calm-and-carry-on 21:03 06.12.2016

25. http://main-riedberg.de/riedberger-stimmen-zum-brexit/ 21:35 06.12.2016